A Hero
Lives in My Family

A Story for Kids of First Responders

By Dr. Susan Hunt
Registered Psychologist

Illustrated by Addie Storm

www.kidsheroseries.com

A Hero Lives in My Family: A Story for Kids of First Responders
Copyright © 2015 Susan Hunt Psy.D.

First Edition

First Book in the Kids Hero Series (www.kidsheroseries.com)

All Rights Reserved.

Cover design and illustrations by Addie Storm.

ISBN-13: 978-1514861226
ISBN-10: 1514861224

Dedication

This book is dedicated to my beautiful children, loving husband, supportive family, helpful friends, and all first responders and their families.

In Loving Memory of RCMP Cpl. Leif Olson, Flight Lt. Jack Hunt (Royal Canadian Air Force, 410 Sqdn), and Cpl. Laurel Hunt (Canadian Women's Army Corps).

To Adrianna and Ella

I have a special story for you;

listen carefully because it's true.

I am a **Helping Hero,**

and I live in this family with you!

As a **Helping Hero** in this world,

I have a story to tell.

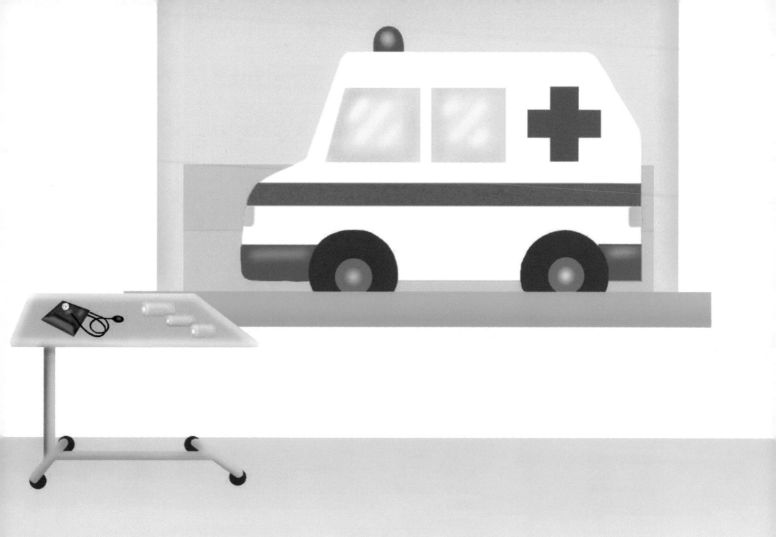

I want to explain my job to you,

      so that you understand it very well.

My helping powers give me strength
to save the people in this world.

I protect, I serve, I help, and I observe.

I listen, I care, and I give hope to people in despair.

I am the first one to respond
when someone is in need.

I try really hard and I love to succeed!

I wear a cool uniform,
and work with people good and bad.

Some of them are happy
and some of them are sad.

Some of them are hurt and need a helping hand.

I am there to make sure they are safe,
and to listen and understand.

I like my job a lot,
because I get to solve problems and do good things.

I love to help others
and see the happiness it brings!

What I want you to know
is that my job is mostly fun.

But sometimes I face danger,
or feel tired before my day has even begun.

Being a Helping Hero can be tough!

Sometimes I have days that are really rough!

I want to tell you about
how my feelings can come about.

Sometimes I feel sad or mad,
and sometimes I may shout.

Sometimes I feel like I want to cry,

Sometimes I have all kinds of feelings inside me,
and I don't know why.

Sometimes I feel sad,
frustrated,
or mad.

But, when I come home to you I feel really glad!

Sometimes my job makes me feel **worried** and scared.

But when I come home and see you,

I feel relaxed and happy

for the time that we have shared!

But I still feel proud,

because I protect, I serve,
I help, and I observe.

When I feel upset,
    or am dealing with something that is bad,

I see your smiling face and no longer feel sad!

Sometimes I feel silly and laugh at funny things,

and let me tell you,
I am always excited about what tomorrow brings!

One of our jobs is helping, saving, and protecting others.

Our other job as Helping Heroes is being fathers and mothers!

As a **Helping Hero,**
my happiest days involve being a parent to you.

I hope you get to see all the ways that this is true!

Let's make a deal to find ways to love

every single day,

Whether we are together, close,

and in the same house, or even far away.

If you ask me what my favorite job is,

please believe me because it's true.

My favorite job in the world
is being a parent to you!

Oh ... and, one last thing I need to tell you:

You are MY Hero,

and I love living in this family with you!

CPSIA information can be obtained
at www.ICGtesting.com
Printed in the USA
LVIC06n1326230718
584641LV00002B/10